For Good Luck!

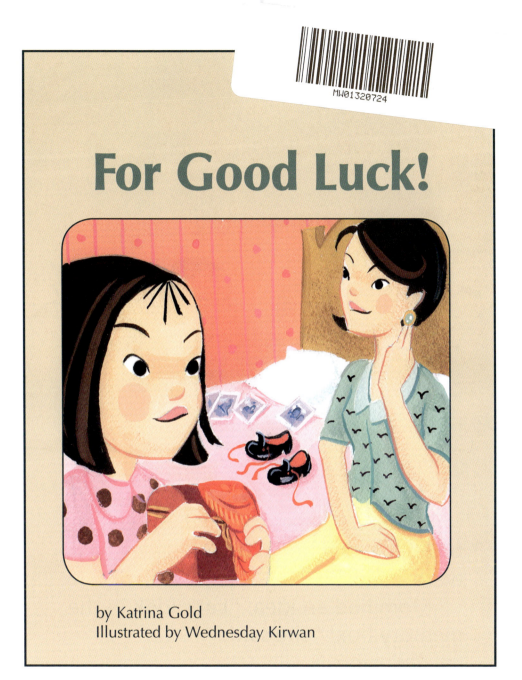

by Katrina Gold
Illustrated by Wednesday Kirwan

Glenview, Illinois • Boston, Massachusetts • Chandler, Arizona
Upper Saddle River, New Jersey

It was a rainy day. Lyn and her brother David had to stay inside. They were bored.

Mom had an idea. "Let's look in the memory box!" she said.

box

Mom used the memory box to keep her treasures, or special things.

Lyn and David liked to look in the memory box. But mostly, they liked the stories Mom told. Mom had a story about each treasure.

---
treasures: valuable things

Mom unpacked the memory box on the bed. She took out each treasure and put it on the blanket. Lyn looked at a little red box. David picked up a small cloth bag.

Lyn asked, "Mom, is this box for earrings?"

Her mother smiled. "Yes," she said. "That case is for the earrings I'm wearing right now."

"Tell us the story of the earrings again!" begged Lyn.

"These earrings belonged to my mother, your Grandma Liu," Mom began. "My father gave them to her. This happened in China, when they got married. Your grandfather said the earrings were for good luck."

"When I left China to come to the United States, I was very unhappy," Mom explained. "Grandma Liu gave me these earrings. She said they would help me feel better. One day I will give them to you, Lyn."

Mom opened the cloth bag. There was a piece of jade inside. "This is Grandpa's stone from China. One day I will give it to you, David."

The children smiled. Outside, it kept raining. But inside the treasures, and their stories, shone like the sun!

---

jade: a hard, green stone